3·95

WHO HUNG THE MONKEY?

(A HARTLEPOOL LEGEND)

by

PAUL SCREETON

CONTENTS

Published by Printability Publishing, Wolviston.
Designed, Typeset and Printed by Atkinson Print Ltd., 10/11 Lower Church Street, Hartlepool,
Cleveland, TS24 7DJ.
First Edition August, 1991.
© Copyright
ISBN 1 872239 06 4

Question: "Is this where they hung the monkey?"
Answer: "Why, have you lost your father?"

PREFACE AND INTRODUCTION

It is quite amazing that no one has previously set down in book form the various stories behind Hartlepool's monkey legend. It cannot be for lack of interest nor for a wealth of background information. There is plenty to say about this dubious event in the history of the Hartlepools.

I hope I have captured the flavour, background, context, nuances and general spirit of the legend. It is presented here in its various guises, along with other local lore and versions from elsewhere of the monkey legend.

It would be presumptuous to believe I have examined every aspect of the legend and I would welcome readers' comments (constructive, preferably) on any aspects of the legend; either counter-arguments, additions or general comment. I can assure readers I will note their points carefully and perhaps a subsequent edition will allow for additions. Correspondents wishing to receive a reply must enclose a s.a.e. and should write to the author at: 5 Egton Drive, Seaton Carew, Hartlepool, TS25 2AT.

But what makes you think I'm a Frenchman?

In former times, mid ear an' strife,
The French invasion threaten'd life,
An' all was armed to the knife,
   The Fisherman hung the Monkey, O!
The Fisherman, wi' courage high,
Siezed on the Monkey for a spy;
"Hang him!" says yen; says another, "He'll die!"
   They did, and they hung the Monkey O!
They tried every means to mych him speak;
They tortor'd the Monkey till loud he did speak:
Says yen, "That's French," says another, "it's Greek"
   For the Fisherman had got druncky, O!
"He's all ower hair!" sum chap did cry,
E'en up te summic cute an' sly;
Wiv a cod's head then they closed an eye,
   Afore they hung the Monkey, O!

Hammer his ribs, the thunnerin thief!
Pummel his pyet weel wi yor neef!
He's landed her for nobbut grief
   He's aud Napoleon's uncky, O!
Thus to the Monkey all hands behaved;
"Cut off his whiskers!" yen chap raved;
Another bawles out "He's never been shaved"
   So commenced to scrape the Monkey, O!
They put him on a gridiron hot,
The Monkey then quite lively got,
He rowl'd his eyes tiv a' the lot;
   For the Monkey agyen turned funky, O!
Then a fisherman up te Monkey goes,
Saying "Hang him at yence, an' end his woes!"
But the Monkey flew at him and bit off his nose
   An' that raised the poor man's Monkey O!

THE FISHERMEN HUNG THE MONKEY

The fate which befell an innocent Monkey, captured many years ago by the Fishermen for a French Spy

Series of three postcards reproduced by kind permission of CLEVELAND WHOLESALE STATIONERS

CHAPTER ONE

MONKEY AS NAPOLEONIC SPY

THE most popular and widespread belief regarding the Hartlepool legend, and which is so deeply rooted that no amount of coercion or reason will shift, is that during the time of the Napoleonic Wars a monkey was washed ashore and mistaken for a French spy. Chattering away and dressed in military-style uniform – as was and sometimes still is such common practice for pets – it was decided that as a precaution it should be hanged.

However, as we shall see, the monkey's appearance could be by way of two means – and anyway it may have been a boy, and not a monkey.

SHIPWRECKED MONKEY
Thomas Hood's account

A most descriptive scenario of events claims to be a "first-hand" account told by Thomas Hood.

Writing in the Northern Daily Mail, James Harrison, then of 81 Lister Street, Hartlepool, reported the shipwreck as related by his maternal grandfather.

Thomas Hood was present as a boy when during a December day early in the 19th century, a heavy gale was raging, thick with snow and the wind in the north-easterly quarter. A large French privateer, Chasse Maree, was spotted during a lift in the weather, bound southwards and close to the Heugh.

Apparently the captain had seen the danger at the same time and the likely peril of his becoming embedded on the treacherous Longscar Rocks, under his lee. He put his helm down, shook two reefs out of the mainsail and headed seaward, close hauled on the port tack. Shortly after making this manoeuvre, the mainsail split from head to foot, took a heavy sea broad on the port quarter, which smothered her and she foundered.

Here we have a great deal of keen observation and technical detail to whet the appetites of Napoleonic theory supporters.

There have been many speculative accounts of the monkey's land-fall, but we may as well continue with the supposed first-hand account – grandson Harrison calls it such, but it must by logic be "second hand" as he's paraphrased it and anyway I've reworded it.

But back with Mr. Hood's eyewitness account. He says that in due time wreckage was washed ashore. Such would naturally be welcome pickings for the fishing community. The spoils from the warship included a piece of wreckage to which hung a bedraggled, shivering monkey.

The fishermen caught the creature – be it scared of them or thankful for rescue or both - and chose to hold a "lobster-pot court martial". The verdict was that the unfortunate beast was a French spy.

Not surprisingly the penalty for spying was death and a coble's mast with halliard rove was erected on the Fish Sands. It was there the monkey was hanged.

Following this, the fishermen visited their usual haunt, the public house which then stood on or very near the Fish Sands, and drank confusion to the French and themselves into more confusion.

A telling conclusion to the tale from grandson Harrison urges: "It behoves all of us who are descendants of the fishermen who hung the monkey to feel proud of our forebears who did their little bit to round up the "little corporal"."

This jibe at the monkey's expense is most revealing. In my mind it cheapens the authenticity of the tale (so much detail seemed sufficiently suspect). For, of course, the "little corporal" reference can only have been to a certain ambitious Herr Adolf Hitler.

The item appeared in the Northern Daily Mail on February 11, 1944, and so must be viewed in its historical and sociological context. Spies, invasion fears, xenophobia, Vichy government; it must have been a period rife with rumours and a classic time for an element of such folklore to surface. Whether factual, fanciful, embellished or a hoax, who knows 140 years after the event, and not knowing how old Harrison was when he wrote it, or whether his faculties were in order. As every folklorist knows, wars and invasion scares are rich breeding grounds for dissemination of rumours and generation of urban belief tales.

The item from Mr. Harrison was challenged immediately by a Mail contributor who went under the pen-name John O'Heugh. "Local historians have never given it credence," he pooh-poohed. He went on: "I cannot seriously accept the story as told in last Friday's 'Mail' by Mr. Harrison. I would imagine any monkey found floating on a spar from a wrecked ship would be of a small breed and common as a ship's pet, and I therefore decline to think that our ancestors were daft enough to hang an innocent little monkey, whose size would not qualify him as a French spy."

John O'Heugh was later to cat-call Harrison as Jim O'Bluff in the Mail.

"X" marks the spot

Harrison may have been bowed by this, but not unbeaten he broached the subject again two years later in the Mail's columns. Apparently a sketch was reproduced of planned redevelopments and he

2

suggested a suitable mark in concrete be erected on the exact position where the coble's mast was stepped to hang the monkey. He added: "May I further suggest that the cost be paid only by the descendants of those fishermen whose vigilance gave a French spy his just deserts (sic)?" He even had "a cross-bearing taken from the shore to the sea ends of the old 'Peggy' pier, which I have stowed away among my records." Sadly, no doubt, these are lost to posterity.

Another Hartlepudlian claiming to know where the hanging took place on the Fish Sands is Ernie Dring, whose grandfather showed him the exact spot around 1927. Mr. Dring pointed it out on television in the B.B.C. programme "Fax" in 1987. This children's show featured a number of local legends (see also Chapter Six).

Ernie Dring on the Fish Sands
Photo by courtesy of The Mail, Hartlepool

Napoleon's ambitions

Going back in time and across the English Channel, it was high taxation which led to the ordinary people of France rising up against the monarchy of Louis XVI. We know this period as the French Revolution.

Utilising the troubles of the time, Napoleon Bonaparte worked to make himself master of France and he set out to conquer Europe.

Naturally at the beginning of the 19th century there was great apprehension among the populace of this small island that the French had hostile intentions towards Britain. A contingent of his armies assembled for more than a year upon the heights above Boulogne.

But as we know from popular history, Horatio Nelson destroyed his invasion fleet at Trafalgar in 1805. Undeterred, Napoleon turned eastwards, brought the countries of Europe under his control and in 1812 invaded Russia. However, the Russians set fire to their capital, Moscow, and forced his retreat. The British under Wellington finally defeated this skilful general at Waterloo in 1815.

Luckily for Britain he was no admiral. He might have known when every horse in a cavalry regiment had to be reshod, and how many loaves a field bakery could turn out in a day, but he knew as little about ships as the designer of the Titanic.

French ship's identity

For those who would favour the Napoleonic spy argument for the legend's genesis, the proven shipwreck of the aforementioned French privateer would surely give heart.

Columnist John M. Ward related in the Hartlepool Star, during 1989, how he followed up Harrison's reference to the Chasse Maree, by writing to the French Maritime Museum, seeking assistance on the vessel's existence. He was referred to the French National Archives, in Paris, but being unacquainted with the language gave up.

Nevertheless he came across Gary Robinson, of the Community Enterprise Trust, whose records containing details of Napoleonic war-ships suggested four vessels with names similar to the Chasse Maree, but there was no record of where they sank. Gary tried to gain more facts from the French National Archives but failed to receive a reply.

No doubt tongue-in-cheek, John M. Ward concluded: "Does this silence mean that even after this period of time the monkey's mission was so dastardly that no information can be divulged as to what it entailed. We will never know."

MENAGERIE ESCAPE

"Sober Truth"

Doubtless the book which contains the alternative Napoleonic version is rare; at least this writer has failed to locate a copy. Hence we must take the accounts of Hartlepool historian John O'Heugh into consideration.

The shorter reference from 1944, in reply to James Harrison's claims, tells us that during the time of the threatened invasion of England by Napoleon, the first big anthropoid ape was introduced by a travelling showman.

O'Heugh puts the book he has referred to as published 'a few years ago', i.e. late 1930s, and names it as "Sober Truth", by Osbert Sitwell and Margaret Barton.

The story goes that a huge ape escaped and roamed the countryside for a few days before its capture in Hartlepool. As no one could understand the beast's grimaces and gibberings, it was consequently tried and hanged as a French spy.

O'Heugh believes the tale can be somewhat substantiated by the fact that at the time Wombwell's Menagerie was touring various fairs and probably visited one at Hartlepool on St. Lawrence's Day, August 10.

This menagerie had played an important role in the history of Hartlepool. It was sufficiently well known to have been visited twice by Queen Victoria, and was previously patronised by King George III, King George IV and Queen Adelaide.

Nowadays whenever alien animals, such as lions, tigers and other large cats, kangaroos or other such exotic fauna as apes and so on are spotted in rural or urban areas, suspicion generally falls on zoos or circuses as having "lost" animals. Wombwell's Menagerie seems an early suspect for this twilight subject of out-of-place beasts.

No doubt the Hartlepool monkey was not contemplating his seminal role for Fortean research, though Sitwell and Barton cogitate: "One wonders what dim consciousness of events passed in the mind of the ape as he swung from the gibbet among the acclamation of the crowd."

REASON FOR DOUBT

North-East England is rich in folklore and tales of supernatural manifestation. The Lambton Worm is the best-known and most complete dragon legend, while the North York Moors was home to the Gytrash of Goathland and Hob of Farndale, while Wade created his supernormal causeway across the heather and on the coast was captured the Merman of Skinningrove.

Any legend of monkey-hanging at Hartlepool should certainly match the latter coastal narrative in folklore annals. But did it?

The Stockton printer and poet Henry Heavisides deplored the fact that south-east Durham had little to boast of in comparison with the stories of dragons, giants and fairies' doings in the regions around.

He found nothing worth mentioning in the Hartlepool district when writing on the subject in 1840. This must seem odd when we consider that at the turn of the century Hartlepool should have become famous as the spot where a monkey was supposedly hanged. If this cannot be considered worthy legend material, then any collector who missed it was not worth his salt. Or did Heavisides consider it historical truth, therefore consigning it to fact, not fiction; reality not legendary unrealism?

But if it is to be considered a literal lynching, should it not have also been recorded in histories of Hartlepool? Surely it would be the highpoint of events during Napoleonic times.

CHAPTER TWO

AQUATIC MONKEY BUSINESS

AS we have seen, documentation of the monkey-hanging legend from the Napoleonic period speaks volumes by its absence.

To find the earliest publication regarding it we must go forward to the 1840s, where a tantalising reference is made in a political pamphlet to "aquatic monkies."

It would seem that this is an oblique reference to "jenny hanivers", showground fakes created to fool the curious and naive into believing they represent a species half-fish and half-monkey.

RAILWAY RIVALRIES

Accounts of the historical development of railways throughout the North-East rarely touch on the intense rivalries which were stirred. As this element of competition is central to a major theory to explain the monkey-hanging legend, it will be necessary to give the background to the early development of rail traffic in the Hartlepools.

By the early 1830s a serious plan had been mooted to create an improved port at Hartlepool to ship coal from the newly-developed South-East Durham coalfield. As each relied upon the other, the undertaking took the name Hartlepool Dock and Railway Company. Tolls on coal down the 23 miles of track from Haswell, via Thornley and Wingate, were high but port dues were cheap. The railway opened in 1835 and was an immediate success, with ships able to enter, load and leave on the same tide. By 1841 the company was carrying more coal than any other railway in the North of England.

Realising the Hartlepool company was contemplating an extension from Wingate to Byers Green to capture its coal traffic from the Clarence Railway, Christopher Tennant projected the Clarence and Hartlepool "Union" Railway, later known as the Stockton and Hartlepool Railway. This envisaged connecting the Clarence line at Billingham with an eight-mile line to the cheaper port at Hartlepool. By this action, the rival railways would be once more on equal terms; shorter mileage of one being balanced by the cheaper tolls of the other and both would use the same port.

In 1837 an Act of Parliament was obtained for the eight miles connection between the Wingate and Byers Green branches, but the Stockton and Hartlepool prospectus was not issued until the following year. This stated that the new railway would communicate with a "new dock to be formed in or adjoining the Slake at Hartlepool."

In a move designed to circumvent a rival port company competing with it, the Hartlepool Dock and Railway Company bought up the Middleton estate on the opposite side of the channel to its unfinished East Dock, consequently securing the entrance to the harbour and all the land on the seaward side of the Slake (a large area of tidal basin and mudflats between Middleton and the Headland).

The H.D.&R.C. issued a pamphlet deploring the plan, but after bitter arguments a compromise was reached, whereby the Stockton and Hartlepool owners agreed to drop the plan for their own dock and instead make use of the other's installations when completed. Stockton trains veered inland to the western shore of the Slake and then accompanied the road over the sluice gates and under the staiths to Hartlepool station.

However, there was a catch to this compromise.

Since 1835 trains had approached Hartlepool from the north by way of Crimdon embankment and were able to complete their journey on high coal staiths. From the south, Stockton trains arrived at the level of the wharves and wagons had to be drawn up at Throston Engine House to the level of the staiths. The charge for this was 3d a ton and this fee cost the collieries a 1d a ton more than it would have cost to take the northerly line.

Hence Clarence supporters were dissatisfied; equally Hartlepool shareholders who doubted the extra export coal would compensate the £30,000 that the dock improvements were to cost. Nevertheless the Stockton and Hartlepool Railway opened in 1840 and its passenger terminus was opposite what was the Richardson Westgarth plant, continuing around the margin of the Commissioners' Harbour into Hartlepool.

In 1842 the chief shareholders of the Stockton and Hartlepool Railway revived the idea of having their own dock and not having to pay the engine house fee.

Historian Robert Wood, in the excellent account of these affairs in his book "West Hartlepool", described the Stockton and Hartlepool Railway as "the Trojan Horse of the Clarence Company. If it was not actually within the walls of Hartlepool, it was just outside."

The three-year agreement was not renewed and on May 23, 1844, the Stockton and Hartlepool Railway obtained an Act of Parliament enabling it to construct its own harbour and dock under the title of the Hartlepool West Harbour and Dock Company. The following August, the Clarence Railway was leased to the Stockton and Hartlepool Railway for 21 years.

"Such was the birth of West Hartlepool," wrote Robert Wood, "an act of aggression against the Hartlepool Dock and Railway Company."

FISHERMEN AND THE FEUD

When the West scheme got underway the excavation of the Coal Dock severed the railway in 1845. A temporary terminus was erected in South Street and then a new station was built opposite Victoria Terrace in 1848 (brick pillars in the otherwise blank wall to the right after crossing the railway at the bottom of Church Street may be its last remnants). Here a row of imposing shops was built and the Ship Inn, later Customs headquarters, and which was reputed to contain the longest bar in England (this story may be apocryphal as I've heard the same claim made for Hartlepool's Travellers Rest). The offices of the West Harbour and Railway Company were also erected.

Additional docks were excavated behind Victoria Terrace and more tracks laid to set trucks to the quayside. Lines were brought around the south end of the terrace and so the street and station were cut off from New Stranton and the rest of the growing town by railway lines. The town was sprouting afresh in Church Street on the opposite side.

Despite the proliferation of railway sidings and burgeoning trade, the towns of Hartlepool and West Hartlepool remained unconnected by rail until 1862, since the Coal Dock enterprise had severed them. Then a new line left the West Hartlepool station in Mainsforth Terrace to pass behind the northern side of Church Street, run parallel with Clarence Road, turn east towards Middleton and went down the old Middleton Road until entering Middleton and following the old route to Hartlepool.

The restoration of a rail link hardly healed the wounds. What began as a battle for survival between the two go-ahead railway companies became a feud whose reverberations are still felt 150 years on. Of course, any intelligent person realises the ridiculous rivalry occurred a century and a half ago, but there are still fiercely partisan people who will wish the communities were still separate. There are Headlanders who bewail the Heugh's plight in the local newspapers' letters columns, feeling they receive less than their fair share of attention and poll tax payers' money. Equally there are West Hartlepudlians who feel Crofters are poor relations and deservedly so.

Amalgamation of the boroughs in 1967 did little to bring the two quarrelling sides together, as the Headland lost its council, court and separate blue buses.

However, there was also animosity between the Headland's native fisherfolk and the railway company and its navvies, who were creating a new harbour and docks from their romantic moorings, which had existed since mediaeval times. Previously, too, they had done without proper elected authority and carried on in a spirit of sturdy self-reliance.

Hence it was that in 1844, with the Stockton and Hartlepool Railway Bill before Parliament, that the proprietors across the Slake had not only the rival railway to contend with but a surly local population.

A campaign to enlist the goodwill of the fishermen then got under way, for there is evidence from a pamphlet of February 8, 1844, that some of the natives had already expressed their approval of the West Dock scheme.

Meetings, placards, petitions and counter petitions, pamphlets for and against poured from the presses, from studied reasoning to downright abuse.

AQUATIC MONKIES

It is, perhaps, from this pamphlet war that the monkey tale has its true genesis. An unusual bill from this period appears to be the earliest documentary reference which could be attributed to the legend.

The document is a small bill, unusually for the period printed in red.

Historian Robert Wood presumed that the initials stood for the Hartlepudlians who favoured the West Dock scheme.

NOTICE.

EXTRAORDINARY CAPTURE.

The Public are respectfully informed that a New Species of Amphibious Animals just caught in the West Dock at Stranton, called AQUATIC MON-KIES, will be exhibited this evening, in the Market Place, between the hours of 4 and 8 o'clock. The Creatures are as tame as Sucking Pigs, and answer to the names of V. B. B. W. O. L. H. F. R. J. J.

J. PROCTER, PRINTER, UNION PLACE, HIGH STREET, HARTLEPOOL.

An even odder notice refers to that other protagonist in this battle of words and wits, a Fisherman.

HURRAH! HURRAH!

Victory ! The show of the monkies did not take place tonight in consequence of the animals being rather unmanageable. But tomorrow night will be seen in the Market Place a Fisherman trying on a new suit, and will at the same time read his Will stating that he may never return alive from London. That his likeness will be taken by the Stockton and Hartlepool Railway for services performed. The Performance to commence at 7 precisely no mistake.
The Public may rely that they will not be disappointed.

Wood's conclusion is that the Fisherman was bribed by the Stockton and Hartlepool Railway Company to give evidence in London in favour of the West Dock. This would explain his new suit, reference to services performed and reason for being held up to public ridicule.

The role of the fishermen seems somewhat ambiguous. They would, it seems, have nothing to gain from either railway undertaking.

It would be the selfish shareholders in the earlier venture in Hartlepool who had greatest reason to fear the West Dock competition, neither fishermen, original inhabitants of Hartlepool or West Dockers, many of whom had migrated from Hartlepool anyway.

By an act of superb irony, the tireless but not entirely honest entrepreneur George Hudson, the "Railway King," extended his empire by making a provisional agreement with the Hartlepool Dock and Railway Company for lease and purchase of its railway and docks.

Hudson and his co-directors in the York and Newcastle Company personally travelled by special train from Ferryhill to take formal possession on October 12, 1846. It was almost a year until the West Dock opened, creating the prosperity on which West Hartlepool flourished.

JENNY HANIVERS

I doubt that the "aquatic monkies" involvement is a red herring. It is more suggestive that one side in the pamphlet war regarded the West Dockers as charlatans and their scheme an enterprise of dubious honesty.

My argument rests on identifying the "aquatic monkies" as "jenny hanivers."

10

These mermaid-type creations were popular last century and a number from that era remain in private hands and public collections. I will describe one I saw in 1980 in a glass case kept then at The Plough public house, Allerdean, near Berwick-upon-Tweed.

It was half-fish, half-monkey and for some reason named Sally! It was about 18 inches long with downy growth all over the head from cranium to chin, and had an Adam's apple in its slender neck. The face was dark brown and somewhat akin to that of a monkey, having small teeth with the longer ones at the front, an apparently built-up nose and false eyes which were extremely lifelike.

The torso was ribbed and long, slender arms extended outwards with narrow fingers with proper nails. These were not webbed. There were no gills, but it had been suggested the nostrils could be used for breathing.

There was no discernible join between torso (seemingly devoid of mammary glands – another argument against femaleness) and the rear half, which resembled a fish. It had dorsal, ventral and pelvic fins, but no pectoral fins.

Oddly its custodian, licensee Mrs. Margaret Harvey, said that since she had been in possession of it, the caudal (tail) fin had continued to grow!

Newspaper cuttings she showed me revealed various discrepancies to Sally's origin.

An undergraduate from a UFO society at Cardiff University had even alarmed Mrs. Harvey with his opinion that such creatures arrived here by extraterrestial craft. "Watching Dr. Who made me uneasy," she told me. "I'd think, what will happen if one of Sally's brothers or sisters come back to see her?"

Mrs. Harvey hoped arrangements could be made to have Sally X-rayed to authenticate her, as she was well aware such prodigies were deftly created by unscrupulous and greedy showmen for exhibition in the past. Sally, however, according to one account had been caught in the sea off Japan.

Peter Dance, in his book "Animal Fakes and Frauds", noted that such a mermaid had been X-rayed and "showed a complicated arrangement of wires which supported the body but failed to support the credibility of this charming mermaid."

An engraving of the "very capital" mermaid seen by Frank Buckland at the Oriental Warehouse of Messrs Farmer and Rogers, as depicted in his book "Curiosities of Natural History", and which is strikingly similar to other jenny hanivers in existence today.

The bill announcing Hartlepool's "aquatic monkies" was printed in 1844. In 1842 we know the celebrated American showman, Phineas Taylor Barnum, who originated W. C. Fields' oft-quoted line "Never give a sucker an even break", at least had the honesty to describe his curio as "an ugly, dried-up, black-looking, and diminutive specimen." After much media-hype, creating an atmosphere of excitement, Barnum exhibited his mermaid. New Yorkers turned up in their thousands to pay 25 cents a head for the privilege of looking at this taxidermitological prune. It transferred to a museum, where takings shot up to 3,500 dollars a month.

Barnum's specimen, by his own admission, was hardly distinguished sounding and he also took note of a naturalist to whom he showed it, who assured Barnum of the origin of the species, i.e. it was fraudulent.

Dating from the last century, examples which appear these days are generally in dilapidated condition. In 1987, Hartlepool's Gray Art Gallery and Museum sent an example for restoration to Newcastle University. Antiquities expert Hazelle Page found it had boreholes created by the ravages of insects and its fins had been broken off. Fish teeth had been utilised to add to its frightening appearance and birds' feet added to produce claws.

The jenny haniver is back again and can be seen in the display case representing the museum in the West Hartlepool Athenaeum during the seven years William Hutton was responsible for it, 1853-1860. Its origin is associated with a bizarre theory of evolution in the text accompanying the display.

To an extent, it seems, the "art" of creating a jenny haniver has not been lost – at least in Hartlepool. An anonymous correspondent to The Mail, Hartlepool, letters page stated that a jenny haniver is a type of small skate, well known to anyone connected with the Fish Quay. These can apparently be folded up, smoked and they then take on the appearance of a small monkey. The writer added that such

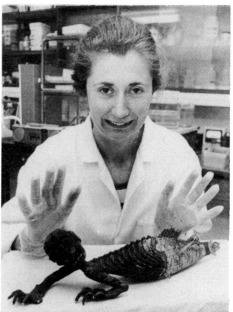

Antiquities conservator for the North of England Hazelle Page with a Hartlepool jenny haniver in 1987, sent for restoration.
Photo courtesy of The Mail, Hartlepool.

was demonstrated on a stall on Lifeboat Day in 1982. Thus there may be an unbroken tradition of jenny hanivers, or "aquatic monkies", in Hartlepool spanning 150 years.

Another living aspect of the monkey legend.

CHAPTER THREE

NED CORVAN'S LOCAL EPICS

Comic songs.

THE 19th century produced a crop of provincial songwriters and balladeers. One such was Edward (Ned) Corvan (1829-1865), and who as a youngster ran off with a group of strolling players.

From the fairground booth, Ned graduated to the music room in the early Victorian public houses. In fact, he went on to become a landlord himself in South Shields and according to posterity, he died of drink.

After his death, admirers of his work and other Tyneside writers and singers, were collected in volumes of songs and poems. It is from such an anthology of fragments that the monkey-hanging legend story and song comes.

However, Corvan's Hartlepudlian song requires placing in context; both how he came to write it and likely inspiration from earlier songs, no doubt familiar to him.

Firstly, Corvan's policy was to dis-cover some local minor disturbance and extend it into an epic. This he would declaim with suitable gestures and those dramatic asides so essential to music-hall gatherings when everyone was merry.

For instance, Corvan related an oc-casion when the Newcastle police force found some Irishmen too much for them to handle, but the native criminals joined in on the side of their traditional adver-saries to rout the foreigners, proving blood can be thicker than water. That particular happening is immortalised as the "Battle of Sandgate". Another tale he wrote was of "The Greet Bulldog O' Shields".

NED CORVAN

13

The Hartlepool legend is known to have been written by Corvan, who died in 1865. After running away from home he eventually joined Billy Purvis's company. He was very fond of the old showman clown, who is buried in St. Hilda's churchyard on the Headland.

The grave of Billy Purvis, where the headstone is considerably worn by the ravishes of time and climate

Billy Purvis as clown at his Victoria Theatre

While with Purvis he made a grand reputation for himself with his popular songs with local themes and delivered with good-natured invective.

After the death of Purvis in December, 1853, Corvan wrote to the Hartlepool printer John Proctor, of Union Place, High Street. In the letter he reminisced of the happy days of his boyhood in Hartlepool and it is apparently obvious he had not been near Hartlepool for many years. (Keith Gregson claims in his book, "Corvan," that he was a Liverpudlian by birth).

His intention in writing the letter was to ask Proctor to make arrangements to stage an entertainment which Corvan had devised about the life and exploits of the well-loved showman.

This all-important letter, which was the property of historian Robert Wood, was unfortunately not dated. However, as Purvis died on December 16, 1853, and Procter himself died in August, 1860, it can only have been written between those years.

It is only speculation, but we may assume that Corvan visited Hartlepool before the performance organised by Proctor seeking a local theme to give topicality to his act.

Robert Wood has suggested a plausible scenario for the discovery of his parochial parody.

We are back now in West Hartlepool with a remarkable event. West Hartlepool mentor Ralph Ward Jackson was the chief promoter of that oddly-formed edifice Christ Church. There was a falling out between the first vicar, John Hart Burges, and when the incumbent refused to come to heel, Jackson had his bricklayers seal up the church doors so that the parson could not enter his church.

From then on until the early days of the 20th century, when election meetings became heated, barrackers and hecklers would be hurling insults. Behind the electioneering and catcalls would be heard a steady bass tone of "Who bricked up the church doors?"

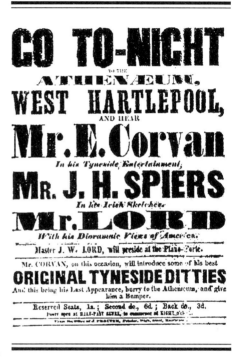

GO TO-NIGHT
TO THE
ATHENÆUM,
WEST HARTLEPOOL,
AND HEAR
Mr. E. Corvan
In his Tyneside Entertainment;
MR. J. H. SPIERS
In his Irish Sketches,
Mr. LORD
With his Dioramaic Views of America;
Master J. W. LORD, will preside at the Piano-Forte.
Mr. CORVAN, on this occasion, will introduce some of his best
ORIGINAL TYNESIDE DITTIES
And this being his Last Appearance, hurry to the Athenæum, and give him a Bumper.
Reserved Seats, 1s.; Second do., 6d.; Back do., 3d.
Party may sit at HALF-PAST SEVEN, to commence at EIGHT o'clock.

A bill publicising one of Ned Corvan's West Hartlepool appearances.

Wood suggested that over the ferry on the Headland a similar sort of slogan would be shouted, only it would take the form of "Who hung the monkey?" He believed Corvan seized on this as his basis for a comic song.

Probably he heard this in 1854 or 1855, but ten years is no time at all in popular culture. The song concluded:

"Still you may hear to this day"

"Boys crying, Who hung the Monkey, O."

Those ten years would take us back to the docks feud, "aquatic monkies" and a contemporary play.

JACK ROBINSON AND PUG

We must return now to the railway rivalry and some possible connections.

The Hartlepool Railway and Dock Company had as its engineer a well-respected man called Stephen Robinson. At that time there was a very popular play called "Jack Robinson and his Monkey". Robert Wood put the two together and suggested that irreverent Crofters proclaimed "We have Jack Robinson on our side of the water. The fellow planning the other dock is the monkey".

Did the "aquatic monkies" refer in some way to Robinson's monkey? And what of the other protagonist, the Fisherman?

Wood notes that in the play the monkey's name is "Mushapug" or "Pug" for short. In no dictionary of that time was the word "pug" used in connection with the monkey species. However, Corvan calls it Pug, as in the play.

Who Hung The Monkey?

With his comic genius, fine singing voice and fiddle, Corvan went down a storm in the bawdy and boisterous atmosphere of quayside pubs' music saloons.

Ned Corvan, as Cat-Gut John, the wandering minstrel.

The song "Who Hung The Monkey?" appears in Allan's "Tyneside Songs", published in many editions between 1862 and 1890, and again in 1972, but under the title "The Fishermen Hung The Monkey, O".

The most popular version prints five double verses, but in the 1863 edition there are six double verses. One double verse with the accompanying prose interpolation or "patter" of the entertainer having been deleted for no obvious reason.

However, Corvan's songs for dockside pub audiences were not likely to be suited to the middle-class intelligensia of Victorian England. Consequently the entertainer had to do some cleaning up before his songs were fit to be published.

We know this occurred, for miraculously a tattered printed copy of Corvan's original song survived the years and fortuitously passed into Robert Wood's hands.

The song made its stage debut at the Dock Hotel Music Hall, Southgate, Hartlepool, on an unspecified date. The ballad sheet contends it was greeted with immense applause, but it has also been suggested Corvan was run out of town for performing it.

As for the song, two verses may be deemed unfit for sensitive souls, but for completeness there is no censoring here. It is important for our heritage that Hartlepudlians are aware that the "authorised" version is suspect and that the true original has survived.

Here's the original to be sung to the tune "The Tinker's Wedding".

"In former times when war and strife,
From o'er the channel threatened life,
When all was ready to the knife,
To watch the Frenchmen, funky, O!
Chorus:– Dooram, dooram, dooram, da,
&

The fishermen with courage high
Seized what they though a real French
spy.
Kill him says yan, up with him to die,
They did, and they hung the Monkey,
O!

They tried every move to make him
speak,
They tortured Pug till he loud did speak,
That's French says one, says another
it's Greek,
The Fishermen they got drunky, O!

He has hair all over the wives did cry,
Oh! what un a woman with him would
like;
With fish-guts then they bung'd up his
eye,
Before they hung the Monkey, O!

Now some the Monkey did bewail,
For although DUMB, he had a tale
(tail),
He'd sooner praps have gone to jail,
For Pug was turning funky, O!

The Monkey made some curious mug's
When they shaved his head and clipped
his lugs,
Saying this is't way to save humbugs;
Before they hung the Monkey, O!

Hammer his ribs the thundering thief,
Pummel his peyte weel, man wi' your
neef,
He's landed here for nought but grief,
He's Old Napoleon's uncky O!

To poor Pug thus, all hands behaved,
Cut of his jimmy some fools raved,
Another cries out he's never been
shaved;
Before they hung the Monkey, O!

Then they put him on a grid-iron hot,
The Monkey then quite lively got,
He grinn'd his teeth at all the lot
And roll's his eyes quite spunky, O!

Then a fisherman up to Pug goes,
Saying let's hang him at once to end
his woes,
The Monkey flew at him and bit off his
nose,
Then they off to the Moor with the
Monkey, O!

But let us hope that on the Sea
We'll still maintain our Soverignity,
May France and England long agree,
And never at each other get funky, O!

As regards poor Pug, I've had my say,
And former times have passed away,
Still you may hear to this very day
Boys crying who hung the Monkey, O!

What is not in doubt is that whether Hartlepudlians liked it or not, they had to be resigned to the fact that Corvan had put them on the map.

18

However, it might have been by chance, for Tyneside could boast earlier "monkey stories" and two previous songs featuring the animals, one unequivocally Napoleonic.

Clues to a Tyneside origin have been found by sleuth Keith Gregson. Head of history and also liaison master at Brierton Comprehensive School, Hartlepool, Keith is also a folk song composer and singer. He is additionally author of "Corvan", a study of the Victorian entertainer and his songs (Kemble Press, 1983).

In this book he draws attention to the song "The Sandhill Monkey", which appeared in a collection of Tyneside songs of 1827. Here a keelman was

Keith Gregson with a copy of his book "Corvan".
Photo courtesy of The Mail, Hartlepool.

foolish enough to hold a conversation with a shopkeeper's pet monkey, without realising it was not the tradesman himself.

However, more interesting was another song from the same period, supposedly based on fact, which bears similarity with the Hartlepool monkey. Among the menagerie was a monkey which escaped. Dressed in a uniform, there was discussion as to whether it was a Jew, Cossack, French spy or Bonaparte himself. It appears in "Tyneside Songster" of 1827. It is of key interest so I include it in full.

THE BABOON

SUM time since, sum wild beasts there came te the toon,
And in the collection a famous Baboon,
In uniform drest-if my story you're willin
To believe, he gat lowse, and ran te the High Fellin.
Fol de rol la, &c.

Three Pitmen cam up-they were smoking their pipe,
When straight in afore them Jake lowp'd ower the dike:
Ho, Jemmy! smash, marrow! here's a reed-coated Jew,
For his fyece is a' hairy, an he hez on nae shoe!

Wey, man, thou's a fuil! for ye divent tell true,
If thou says 'at that fellow was ever a Jew:
Aw'll lay thou a quairt, as sure's my nyem's Jack,
That queer luikin chep's just a Russian Cossack.

He's nae Volunteer, that aw ken biv his wauk;
An' if he's outlandish, we'll ken biv his tauk:
He's a lang sword ahint him, ye'll see'd when he turns:
Ony luik at his fyece! smash his byens, how he gurns!

Tam flang doon his pipe, an' set up a great yell;
He's owther a spy, or Bonnypairty's awnsel:
Iv a crack the High Fellin was in full hue an' cry,
To catch Bonnypairt, or the hairy French spy.

The wives scamper'd off for fear he should bite,
The men-folks an' dogs ran te grip him sae tight;
If we catch him, said they, he's hev ne lodging here,
Ne, not e'en a drop o' Reed Robbin's sma' beer.

My interpretation is that of a travelling menagerie, though Gregson suggests a group of friendly Cossacks were paying a visit to Newcastle when a pet baboon escaped while they were ashore and created havoc in the city. A songwriter seized upon the tale to have fun at the expense of local pitmen.

To the tune "Derry, Down", it had other Tyneside songs set to it and so doubtless Corvan knew "The Baboon." The basis for his Hartlepool song is here: mistaken identity, dressed in a uniform, relationship to Napoleon and hairy French spy.

Likely "The Baboon" was grafted on to the events, still fresh in memories, of the railway rivalry. It was the style of this true professional to work this way upon finding a suitable victim for a reworking.

OTHER MONKEY HANGERS

HARTLEPOOL is not unique in having a community which supposedly hung a monkey of dubious origins. The tale ranges from Aberdeenshire to Cornwall and inland to Derbyshire.

BODDAM
The Boddam wreckers

Briefly, the folk of Boddam deliberately lured a vessel on to rocks and had to dispose of the ship's monkey so as to legally claim the cargo. Charming chaps!

According to this version, one dark and stormy night, many years ago but date unspecified, a ship called the Anna went on the rocks of Boddam, a small port in Aberdeenshire and the most easterly point in Scotland. The following morning the villagers waded out and found that the sole survivor was the ship's monkey. They hanged the unfortunate beast from the ship's yardarm, in the belief that otherwise it would be legally entitled to the valuable cargo.

James Drummond

The claim that Boddam rightly had an earlier genesis of the legend than Hartlepool was claimed by James Drummond, who wrote up his claims in The Scots Magazine and two articles for the Mail, Hartlepool (these challenged in 1982 by this writer).

There's nothing wrong with community chauvinism, but the Aberdonian Drummond's claim for "being feggy," as we'd say in Hartlepool, is a gauntlet worth accepting.

He claimed the authentic story came from the Buchan district and dated from the time when there was great rivalry between the town of Peterhead and the village of Boddam on the other side of the bay. Peterhead people had grand houses and fine manners, created by the prosperity which came from the whaling industry and gentility, which lingered on from its days as a fashionable watering resort. They never lost the opportunity to remind the poor fishing community folk of Boddam of their lowly ways and limited intelligence.

Consequently the Boddamers still face jibes about the ill-gained profits. Just as Hartlepudlians are asked "Who hung the Monkey?", a Peterhead man might greet a Boddam fisherman with "Aye, aye, man! Are you looking for a monkey?" To which the standard reply was, "Foo, fit's wrang, man. Hae yer lost yer brither?"

Drummond questioned an old sea dog called Jimmy Cruickshank, who began his seafaring days aged ten on his father's boat. He recalled how as village boys the fisher folk children in games were the in-byes, while the out-byes were the sons of farmers, quarrymen and rope workers. In those days the in-byes always took the seaward side, no matter what way the wind was blowing. Then as with adult soccer match spectatorship, ball games would reach the stage of traditional insults. Replies to references to alleged poverty of the out-byes (for not all lived in those grand houses) would bring the response, "Fa hingit the monkey?"

The herring connection

Napoleon Bonaparte has no place in Drummond's argument, but Stephen Robinson's railway scheme is central to his thesis. He argues that during that confusing period when the West Dock project was being brought to fruition there were occasional street battles. A gang of navvies had been brought over from Ireland to do the heavy work and they became involved in brawling. He also states that "for some reason there seem to be some fisher folk from Buchan in the melee, throwing fish heads at the street urchins and shouting their traditional war cries. It was those Buchan fisher folk who brought the monkey story to Hartlepool."

It was they who during the propaganda war of words supposedly supplied the cultural link. They hung the monkey, they may have introduced new items of "blason populaire" (see chapter 5), they threw the fish heads . . . but what of the herring connection?

Drummond argues with some persuasion that Boddam girls would have more in common with Hartlepool and other North-East England fishing ports than villages ten miles inland from their own hamlet.

During a short fishing season, as the shoals moved south, so the fleets followed them. Each year, around the beginning of July, they would head for the summer spawning grounds to join the local fleets, moving later farther south to Great Yarmouth and Lowestoft.

Fisher girls followed these vessels. There they would work late into the night if there was a good catch, knives flashing in the torchlight as they cleaned and pickled the herring. As the night wore on there would be aggravation as they gaggled on, with rivalry between Blue Mogganers from Peterhead versus the folk from Boddam. There would be fish heads and herring guts sometimes filling the air between rival sections.

But as with playground or sporting language, there would be the fishwives' legendary command of verbal abuse. They would sing:

> *"There was a ship came round the coast*
> *And all the hands on her were lost*
> *Barrin' the monkey on the post*
> *And the Boddamers hanged the monkey o'*
> *Chorus: Derrum a do a do a day*
> *Derrum a do a daddy o'*
> *Derrum a do a do a day*
> *The Boddamers hanged the monkey o'.*

Familiar?

Drummond calls it "a fine old ballad with the rousing rhythm of the call-to-arms in its chorus, especially when you beat it out with a couple of barrel staves on the empty sides of a salt tub." Is this what the fishwives did?

Corvan's piracy?

As for Corvan's immortal song, Drummond even had the audacity to scornfully describe it as an "inferior ballad that blazons" the Hartlepool tale. Unswervingly certain both legend and song originated in Buchan, he regarded it as "a piece of cultural piracy equalled only by the capture of the lovely 'Lili Marlene' by British soldiers in North Africa during the second world war."

And equally vituperatively: "It is a poor, nasty piece of work, with none of the vigorous simplicity of the Buchan from which it was copied." He believed inexpert cobbling of new words to the original rhythm to be seen at its worst in the chorus.

But we have no date for the Boddam version. Nor, have we a name for its creator.

20th century monkey business

Moving swiftly across the years, Drummond brings the story up to date with a couple of 20th century points.

It is said that when in 1936 the film "King Kong" was shown at Peterhead Playhouse, there was a story that the Boddam coastguards had reported seeing the monster striding up the beach at the Lido looking for his brother.

More recently, Drummond claims, during a rabies scare, an anonymous telephone call about animals being smuggled ashore sent a naive auxiliary coastguard around Boddam inquiring if anyone had seen a man with a monkey. "He was a Cruden Bay man and didn't know any better."

At the time of challenging Hartlepool's supremacy for the legend, 1982, Boddam Primary School had officially adopted a chimpanzee at Aberdeen Zoo.

Not guilty

Having rubbished Ned Corvan, Drummond saw fit to whitewash the Boddamers' dastardly act.

He could not believe the kind, friendly folk of Boddam could even in times of hardship have lured ships on to the rocks and murder any survivors for a few kegs of spirits or bales of costly fabric.

Despite elements to promote a flourishing wrecking industry – busy sea lanes, richly-laden sailing ships standing off Kinnaird Head waiting the wind's favours, rocky coastline forming a lee shore in treacherous easterly gales, warning beacons which could be extinguished or moved to attract a ship, poverty ashore – Drummond could find no evidence that Boddamers were so disposed. He claimed Customs and Excise records showed they were always scrupulously honest in surrendering on demand any goods of value which came from such ships.

Gratified, Drummond could not find any clue to what was the embryonic event to create the monkey-hanging legend. Was there ever a ship called the Anna? We are left with another question mark.

Oil bonanza

Boddam, a one-time small and picturesque fishing village is now at the centre of the North Sea oil boom. The local legend now focuses more on this bonanza. It goes like this:

Murphy went for a job on a North Sea oil rig. He walked up to one of the labourers and asked him who the foreman was.

"You'll be wanting to see Paddy," came the reply.

"Where will I find dis fella?" asked Murphy.

"Oh, that's easy," came the reply. "Paddy is the one on the landing pad, feeding bread to the helicopter."

Which brings us to our next aspect, almost – but before that we must drop in on Cornwall and Berkshire.

MEVAGISSEY

Another serious fishing port which has a monkey-hanging legend is Mevagissey, in south Cornwall.

It combines a role of tourist resort during the summer, but its menfolk were once purely engaged in chasing shoals of fish, being particularly famous for its huge catches of pilchards.

It was also famed for its independence and insularity of its inhabitants. They were once supposed to have hanged a monkey which was washed ashore from a shipwreck, and as with Hartlepool, it was supposedly during the Napoleonic Wars and the creature was likewise hanged as a suspected spy.

Happily, they welcome strangers nowadays.

CHALVEY
Stab monk tradition

I thought long and hard as to whether to include this strange tale from Berkshire. However, as will be seen, it may have relevance.

Chalvey is a village near Slough, Berkshire, whose strong identity is emphasised by the pride with which Chalvey men call themselves "stab monks". For here they did not hang a monkey, but one was stabbed to death.

Between 1850 and 1870 there was a colony of Italians living in Thames Street, Windsor, and one Sunday an organ-grinder arrived from there with his monkey to earn a few coppers. He began playing in Chalvey Grove, and attracted a crowd of children. Unfortunately the monkey suddenly bit one of the youngsters who were watching, perhaps because they were teasing it. The child rushed home to tell his (or her – for there are some minor divergences in versions) father, who was sitting down to his supper after a session at the Cape of Good Hope public house. The father, being rather the worse for drink, rushed out and stabbed the monkey to death.

When the organ-grinder lamented his loss, villagers took pity on him and held a collection to buy him another monkey. To finance this they carried the monkey's body around the village and when they had sufficient to replace the unfortunate beast, they buried it in Chalvey Grove and held a "wake" with the money left over.

The following year it was agreed to repeat the "wake" annually. At this a man was chosen each year on Whit Monday to be Mayor of Chalvey and his method of election to office was by being the first Chalvey man to get so drunk he fell into Chalvey Brook or Black Ditch. This mock mayor would then be known as Long John.

The minutiae of the tradition need not concern us, nor local historian Michael Bayley's attractive though far-fetched argument that the ceremonies go back to the religious rites of Dionysius as a seasonal fertility cult. It is, however, perhaps pertinent to draw a couple of parallels with tradition in Hartlepool, particularly the former village of Middleton.

Mayor of Middleton

There is the gruesome demise of a monkey, an unstated but probable underlying xenophobia, and both elect mock mayors.

It is hard to imagine today that this quaint spot, surrounded by industry and about to be swept away by the marina project, was once a cheerful, thriving community and popular picnic rendezvous. About all that's left is the bustling Smallcrafts Club, where each spring they elect a Mayor of Middleton. This mock mayor office was revived in 1970 and the tradition is extremely rare in Britain these days.

Nationally respected folklorist Derek Froome, who collects information on these traditions, told me when I introduced him to Middleton's example: "They are very fugitive and their discovery is more often than not a pursuit of serendipity."

The first of the latest sequence of mayors was Owen Richmond, now a retired union official, who held the office again in 1982, a particular honour as it was also Maritime England Year, and has been mayor no fewer than four times. He has one of the cabins opposite the club and outside, in addition to an anchor from the passenger liner Oslo-fjord, sunk in 1941 off the Tyne, has erected a mock gallows from which he hangs a toy monkey.

This close affinity between two rare mock mayor traditions and the violent death of a monkey may be spurious, but at least we can see community identity as a prominent aspect. It would certainly be interesting to know whether the Middleton tradition was linked to the year, or anniversary, of the monkey-hanging.

Owen Richmond recreates the monkey hanging in Middleton. The mock gallows were erected in 1985 outside his well-appointed and cosy cabin. The legend was reborn in Middleton for its fete. Owen said it should belong as much to Middleton as to the Headland.
Photo courtesy of The Mail, Hartlepool.

BLASON POPULAIRE

ROBERT CHAMBERS wrote more than 100 years ago:
"There is a nationality in districts as well as in countries; nay, the people living on different sides of the same stream, or of the same hill, sometimes entertain prejudices against each other, not less virulent than those of the inhabitants of the different sides of the English Channel on the Pyrenees. This has given rise to an infinite number of phrases, expressive of vituperation, obloquy, or contempt, which are applied to the inhabitants of various places by those whose lot it is to reside in the immediate vicinity. Some of these are versified, and have the appearance of remnants of old songs; others are merely couplets or single lines, generally referring to some circumstances in the history of the subject, which originally called for the ridicule of the neighbours and continues to do so traditionally."

"Blason populaire"

The jibe "Who hung the monkey?" relates as we have seen to Hartlepudlians and Boddamers. The Boddamers also claim joint ownership – or origination of – the catcall "I hear they're painting the end of the new pier red to save lighting a beacon at night" with regard to Hartlepool, whereas there was a claim by their enemies that Boddamers had painted red rings around their lighthouse so that it could be seen in the dark without recourse to a lamp. Also in Sunderland the townsfolk supposedly painted the lighthouse red to save buying oil for the lamp.

These are examples of "blason populaire". It is a simple expression for a distinct form of local tradition, a jeering slogan or jibe, a taunt levelled in semi-malicious fun by the inhabitants of one town or region against those of another.

Back in Buchan, "Did you hear the one about the Boddamer who thinks that it's the mill on Windmill Brae that makes the wind?"

Meanwhile, our Hartlepool ancestors remarked of West Dockers being "all huddled together like the folk of Shields. It was cheaper to build a wall around them than put up a lunatic asylum."

Both at Sunderland and Robin Hood's Bay, residents allegedly threw a canary over the cliff to break its legs.

Further down the coast Bridlington inhabitants are known as Bolliton Jackdaws. It seems the townspeople were anxious to repair their parish church and found it necessary to replace one of the beams across the nave. After making measurements they found a piece of timber suitable for the job and fashioned it into shape and tried to get it into the church.

However, when they tried getting it in the church door they were unsuccessful however hard they tried. Dejected, they were about to give up when a jackdaw was seen to carry a straw in endways to make a nest.

They then went and did likewise. Since that day they have been Bolliton Jackdaws.

Somewhere in Derbyshire

There is also a story that an ape appeared in a remote Derbyshire village. The villagers apparently took it for a Napoleonic spy and he was tried, sentenced and executed. The point of the story, wrote John Michell in "The Flying Saucer Vision", that 19th century English country people could not differentiate between a monkey and a Frenchman, is not to be taken seriously.

Pox, lust and superstition

Another brief tale claims Crofters placed fishing nets across Throston Bridge to keep out smallpox or the plague. There is another tale regarding the building of the Town Wall. This was during the Viking period of rape and pillage – not to keep the Scandinavian seafaring warriors out, but to keep them in, for the seductive licentiousness of the lusty maidens of Queen Street.

As with most communities and professions, Hartlepool fishermen had their superstitions. They would not put to sea on a Sunday and like pitmen farther up the coast, if they met a woman on their way to work, would return home rather than tempt providence. If anyone died, the windows would be hung with white sheets with a black cross in the centre, mirrors in the house would be covered up and other fishermen acted as pallbearers.

Frying bacon, pushing St. Hilda's and a sea serpent

Three rather more substantial tales, at least with more commentary, can be found in Hartlepool's past.

Firstly, after the threat of the Spanish Armada had passed, an edict from Parliament was sent to Hartlepool, instructing that "no more firing should take place at the beacon."

Unfortunately the mayor at the time was illiterate and the message was interpreted by the local schoolmaster (who can't have been too clever himself) as meaning that no further frying of bacon should take place there.

Thereupon the mayor ordered all frying pans be collected and deposited in the churchyard.

Historian John O'Heugh claimed in an article in the Mail that as recently as 1893 a frying pan had been found buried there.

Of course, the reference had been to the beacon a few yards north of the Fairy Cove Battery and the order was designed to stop the guns firing.

Another threat from off the coast lies behind the second tale. Waves' power of denudation lie at the root of another story to mock the credulity of the Headlanders.

In response to the concern of the vicar of St. Hilda's, fishermen were urged to push the church farther inland for safety.

Before attempting this task they took off their coats. While they heaved and grunted at the east end, a passing rag and bone man spotted the garments. Hardly believing his good fortune, he collected them and went on his way the richer.

After awhile, the fishermen went to check their progress, and noting the clothing had disappeared from view, assumed they had pushed the church sufficiently far westwards and inland to have buried their coats.

Our third tale features the fishermen again and puts them in the light of being both wily, acquisitive and not altogether honest.

As the number of visitors to the town increased, the fisherfolk spotted a potential money-spinning idea. There was already the legend of the Lambton Worm inland in County Durham. They may also have known that one of the Castle Eden gentry of the Burdon family, along with companions, had reported she had seen a 200-foot long sea serpent off Blackhall Rocks in September, 1850.

Whatever the genesis, local fishermen would arrange for a small flotilla of cobles in line astern to lie out in the bay, covered in sailcloth and sacking, thus suitably decorated to resemble in some form a serpent. When the taverns closed for the night, offers would be made to take those made brave by liquor out to view the sea serpent – at a price. As they sailed out, a look-out would spot the monster. In the moonlight, the nervous sightseers would see in their excitement what they assumed to be the sea serpent they had heard so much about. By now scared witless, they would demand to be returned with haste to the safety of the shore. Their adventure over, they would be deposited thankfully, while the fishermen would be a little richer.

Foolish or commonsensical

There would seem to be two sides to those blason populaire tales. Seemingly they reveal people within a community as simpletons, but why not see them in a different light?

The largest single body of blason populaire tales is associated with the Nottinghamshire village of Gotham. These generally go under the generic title of the Wise Men of Gotham, suggesting a far from daft populace.

According to legend, the wicked King John planned to establish a hunting lodge in the village, but the local folk did not want anything to do with the evil monarch. Of course, if they raised objections, there was the likelihood he would retaliate. Consequently the villagers devised a system whereby they would all appear simpletons.

When the king's advance party arrived in Gotham, they were presented with a catalogue of tales which implied that the village was populated by idiots. Following this, the king's representatives returned to report the villagers as mad, while the locals congratulated themselves on their cleverness.

The Rev. J. E. Field recorded how the Wise Men of Gotham decided to make the summer last forever in "The Myth of the Pent Cuckoo." They planned to accomplish this by stopping a cuckoo migrating and built a wall around the crown of the hill where it was singing on a tree. When the cuckoo flew over the wall they decided their construction had not been sufficiently tall.

A quack doctor, Andrew Borde, commemorated no fewer than 20 local examples in his 16th century book, "The Wise Men of Gotham." For instance they also had problems with an eel which ate all the fish in the village pond, so they caught it and threw it into the river to drown it. Then the village blacksmith had problems with a nest of wasps in the thatch of his smithy, so he set the roof on fire to burn them out. Then men seeing water bubbling over some rocks thought it was boiling and tried to cook their porridge in it, and when one jumped in to taste it he was drowned.

Also common in Wiltshire, but also located in Gotham, were a couple of variants on moon-raking. A horse-rider paused to allow his steed to drink from a pond, but as the beast drank the moon vanished. Fearing his horse had consumed the moon, he cut his horse in half to release it. Another group on another occasion tried to rescue the moon from the pond by forming a chain to pull it out with a rake.

Many, many more such tales exist, to show varying levels of the ludicrous or commonsensical behaviour among local communities. Hanging the monkey in Hartlepool was a mixture of both.

But let's not forget the blason populaire jibes up in Aberdeenshire. Remember the Boddam claim to originating the monkey legend? Journalist James Drummond first became aware of his local tale when he was at a football match between Peterhead and Fraserburgh in the Thirties. Jobs were scarce and there were no herring in the North Sea. Remember those playground farmers' sons and their alleged poverty? Drummond heard as the Fraserburgh goalie missed an easy save and fell flat on his face: "Dinna eat the grass, mun! Ye'll get your hauf egg for tea!" A Broch supporter responded with: "Fa hangit the monkey?"

As seen, variations on a theme exist in Hartlepool, Boddam, Mevagissey and inland Derbyshire. If blason populaire is one form of folklore, then urban belief tales are another. These tend to attach themselves to rites of passage, cars and caravans, sexual mischief and also to an extraordinary extent, food and animals. To end this chapter on a bizarre note, in Holland, urban legends are known as broodje aap, or translated "monkey sandwiches," with reference to the story that certain sausages are made of monkey meat.

MONKEY HANGING IN MODERN TIMES

THE legend's association with "modern" times could be regarded as beginning with the Jubilee celebration in Hartlepool in 1887 ending with a grand display of fireworks on the Town Moor. The highlight was a set-piece showing the monkey hanging on a rope. As the closing sequence it was made to buzz around ablaze and the crowd did not appreciate the spectacle one bit.

The spread of the tale was greatly enhanced in the 1890s when Hartlepool Rovers were having a glorious period and hung a stuffed monkey from the rugby field crossbar before a match. National newspapers reported this behaviour and no doubt people's movements during two subsequent world wars did much to perpetuate the story.

Today it is still commonly known when Hartlepudlians announce their hometown to strangers.

Still making news

Hartlepool's local newspaper, The Mail, has reported in words and pictorially many stories about the monkey-hanging legend. These have ranged from erudite articles on the origin of the legend to an April Fool's Day spoof in 1986.

There have been stories about the legend's depiction in brick by building apprentices, its reproduction in wood as part of an animated clock for a Middlesbrough shopping centre, where the monkey was to be unceremoniously hung 24 times a day. There was even a team from the British Sugarcraft Guild, whose tasty tableau of the legend was modelled, painted and

Norma Kilburn (left) a and Sylvia Bantoft, Hartlepool members of the British Sugarcraft Guild with their tableau.
Photo courtesy of The Mail, Hartlepool.

glazed entirely from sugar over several months of dedicated work. Their sweet piece de resistance success was "Hanging of the Spy".

Mail centenary

It was Mail employees who took the monkey as a theme and made news themselves when they entered the annual Harbour Fete raft race. More then 10,000 people turned out to watch the event and minutes before the race was due to start they were treated to the sight of a monkey drifting in the bay on a raft. The Mail's raft, suitably decorated to celebrate the newspaper's centenary that year, 1977, was in hot pursuit and captured the monkey. Landed on the beach, the monkey was promptly arrested by three Mail employees masquerading as real officers, who marched him up the beach to where the hangman was waiting beside some gallows. However, much to the delight of waiting children, the monkey struggled free and escaped. The effort won for The Mail the trophy for most entertaining raft.

"Monkey" Clive Kerfoot is taken into custody by (left to right) Gerry Scanlon, Keith Midgley and Colin Campbell. (Picture by "hangman" Harry Harland). *Photo by courtesy of The Mail, Hartlepool.*

Council publicises folktales

FOLKLORE AND LEGEND

(AND THEREBY HANGS A TALE)

Hartlepool Borough Council produces pamphlets of local interest and one of these, "Folklore and Legend", features among other tales, the monkey-hanging.

Illustration courtesy of Hartlepool Borough Council

Monkey Hangar Beer

In May, 1989, Hartlepool's Tap & Spile pub held a Monkey Beer Festival at which Monkey Hangar, with an original gravity of 1058 was the strongest ale. "Get rid of all your hang-ups," it was advertised, coming from Bill Witty's Big End Brewery, Harrogate. Landlady Anne Bell reported that the five-day boozy extravaganza attracted 35 different brews and an estimated 1,000 real ale enthusiasts. Best seller was Monkey Hangar and here's the . . .

HISTORY OF THE MONKEY HANGAR

Once upon a time, Bill the home brewer from Harrogate, sat on his firkin thinking. His one ambition in life was to create a beer that would go down in the annals of the drinker's bible, the Good Beer Guide.

Meanwhile, in a little village called Hartlepool, the good wizard Wallbank waved his magic wand and turned the crumbling Causeway into the terrific Tap & Spile. The rejuvenated ex-tenant now became the Manager and as such managed to ring Bill in Harrogate to request a beer be created to celebrate the return of the little hairy man himself.

The Manager, whose name was Anne, managed to board the 9.15am mailcoach at 11.15am and didn't spare the horses until they arrived at the Big End Brewery.

There was an air of great expectancy (being a converted stable, there was a pregnant horse in the corner). The ingredients were carefully inspected and brewer Bill set to work on creating his masterpiece, now known as 'Monkey Hangar'.

Reader, this story is true. I know, I was that pregnant horse. This is straight from the horses mouth.

. . . and the cover of the publicity leaflet:

M O N K E Y   B E E R   F E S T
May
25th-29th

**Just when you thought is was safe
to forget all about him....**

THE HERO IS BACK!

Monkey Hangar!

appearing at

Stranton, Hartlepool.

Fame on TV

Television viewers could spot the name "Hartlepools" on a Brooke Bond tea chimps' advertisement ten years ago. It was one of a series of spoof spy spots showing cheeky chimpanzees.

A chimp spy was about to board the Orient Express, whose destination board read: Whatapest, Dustinhoff, Sofia, Sogood, Nice, Nasty, Hartlepools, Paris.

Apparently scriptwriter Tony Toller was among a team which gave a talk to The Mail's former Women's Circle promotional readership venture. Toller remembered the legend from his successful visit and included it in the television script.

The chimp spy about to embark in 1980 on the transEuropean express in the hope of rescuing the secret plans for brewing Brooke Bond tea.

Food for thought

From tea to costly food. I understand that there was a Hang the Monkey restaurant in London's West End. In fact, in aptly-named Cleveland Street, W1. I say "was" and maybe again "is." For it had been closed after fire damage, but a resourceful fan of Mike Amos' Eating Owt column in the Northern Echo sent a copy of the menu. I reproduce here the cover and on the reverse was a version of our familiar tale. Amos quoted for starters the pricy breakfast prices and added: "Hang that, as they used to say in Hartlepool."

Fanzine fun

Soccer fans' fanzines are a popular phenomenon these days and to their opponents Hartlepool United are still the "Monkey Hangers". A typical fanzine cover poking fun at the Hartlepool fraternity came from Leyton Orient supporters in 1989.

Then midway through the 1989/90 season, Hartlepool United Football Club got the supporters' fanzine it so richly deserved, though three of its prime movers all live in Colchester (whose team was relegated at the end of the season). Named "Monkey Business", it utilises the legend connection, having the editor as Graeme "Mervyn the Monkey" Young and featuring him on the back page in a cartoon with Bruce the Moose.

Issue one was crammed with light-hearted personal acrimony towards club officials, Darlington F.C., soccer in-jokes and fourth-form sex-

JANUARY 1989   No 25

LEYTON 30p
ORIENTEAR

The Alternative Orient Supporter's Magazine

WATCH OUT — HERE COMES . . .

DON'T MENTION THE MONKEY!

POSTPONED DUE TO CONTINUED INTEREST IN THE F.A. CUP — UNLIKE OURSELVES

H A R T L E P O O L

DON'T SAY WE DIDN'T WARN YOU!

LEYTON ORIENT v HARTLEPOOL UTD, LEYTON STADIUM, 28:01:89

36

ist ribaldry. At number six in the "15 good things about Hartlepool and its people", it gives "you are never likely to be strangled by a stray monkey."

Military matters

As noted, two world wars helped spread the monkey story, so it is not surprising that the part-time soldiers of the town's 118 (Tees) Royal Engineers squadron of the Terriers have a toy monkey as their mascot. It goes on exercises with them and was hanging on a mock gibbet when they spent three days building a bridge for the National Garden Festival at Gateshead. However, their counterparts in the Newcastle squad captured it. "We know it was them because they left a calling card," said Lieutenant Dave Ritchie.

And for completeness, I must mention a scrap of information passed to a colleague. Until it was melted down for the Second World War munitions effort, a World War I Tank called Egbert was positioned in Hartlepool's Vicarage Gardens in Stranton district. Margaret O'Rourke was told by a contact that when it was removed, the skeleton of a monkey was found there!

Strange coincidence

Boddamist James Drummond's correspondent T. B. Picknet, a Redcar man, told of a boy who left his employment to go off in S.S. Sedgepool, who when they were sailing up the St. Lawrence estuary, the skipper of a small Canadian boat, identifying the Hartlepool registration mark, blew his hooter in a somewhat rude fashion and pointed to one of his crewmen, who was hanging derisively from the rigging by one hand, making unmistakeable monkey gestures.

Strangely it was St. Lawrence's Day when Hartlepool's Town Moor fair was held and a monkey could have escaped from there from Wombwell's Menagerie.

More musical interludes

Ned Corvan wasn't the only person to write and perform a song about the Hartlepool monkey legend.

In the Twenties, music-hall duo Flotsam and Jetsam sang or spoke this verse:

> *"The Geordies sent a horse bus off to Blaydon.*
>
> *They put a dog, a monkey and little mouse inside.*
>
> *The mouse said they wouldn't stop cos he knew all the rules.*
>
> *The dog too said stop at Scotswood (why?) there's lamp-posts there you fools.*
>
> *The monkey said stop anywhere excepting Hartlepools."*

More recently, internationally-known folk singer Vin Garbutt has a version in his repertoire, "The Hartlepool Monkey Song", having recorded it when he was with Teesside band The Fettlers. It was set to the tune of "The Darkey's Sunday School."

The legend also inspired Manor School music teacher Gavin Smith to compose "Rumba for Monkeyhangers", which received its first public performance by a wind band at Hartlepool's Borough Hall in 1982.

Still on the Headland, a tape, recorded and mixed at the Durham Street Studio in 1984, a collection of numbers by Hartlepool artists, was given the legend-inspired title "Beats Hanging Around."

Trying hard

Never mind that Hartlepool has a club which keeps narrowly avoiding relegation from the Football League, with only occasional successes, the twin former boroughs have a fierce history of rugby rivalry.

Many clubs have associated themselves with the monkey legend, but undoubtedly none so

Vin Garbutt
Photo courtesy of The Mail, Hartlepool.

strongly as Hartlepool Rovers' Football Club, which was formed in 1879, and has had an unbroken existence since then.

From club stalwart Ernie Dring I learned that around the turn of the century a retired seaman used to attend games at the Old Friarage with his live pet monkey. It was attached to a long chain and he would allow it to jump and swing on the crossbar, generally causing hilarity among the crowd, particularly the younger supporters.

Eventually he and his monkey passed away and after a short period another supporter made his own monkey out of hessian, stuffed with straw and sawdust, plus a home-made face. As the season went on it became a form of mascot at games, particularly at cup-ties.

There have been a succession of such entertainers of this kind, and since 1960 Ernie Dring has been known as the custodian of the Rovers' monkey.

For many years the monkey was an unofficial model which clashed cymbals, but today Ernie has a puppet monkey, which he uses on special occasions to amuse youngsters.

Getting your Fax right

The "Fax" programme for children's ITV was filmed all in one day, December 17, 1986, for transmission the following year. It was produced by the redoubtable Sid Waddell and presented with admirable stoicism by the lovely Debbie Rix. Filming ended with shots in the Rovers' bar with opinions on the legend, particularly those of Ernie, who had his puppet attacking Debbie Rix in Rod Hull's Emu style, knocking off one of her earrings.

Monkey on the bus

To end this modern round-up, here's a joke. It would be better told, particularly if the raconteur and audience were in their cups.

A Rovers' team goes to a match at Twickenham with a live monkey as mascot. On the way back to Hartlepool the bus crashes and the only survivor is the monkey. A police officer tries to communicate with the monkey to ascertain what had happened.

Debbie Rix

Eventually he has some success and when asked what was happening at the rear of the coach the monkey makes a gesture indicating people playing cards.

In response to the question of what was happening in the centre portion, the monkey gesticulates as if singing and waving a scarf.

As to those at the front, the money demonstrates the drinking of cans of beer.

When asked about the driver, it holds its hands as if reading a newspaper.

Lastly, the police officer, asks what the monkey was doing itself. Its hands move as if controlling the steering wheel . . .

CONCLUSION

So what, if anything, really happened? Was a monkey hanged in Hartlepool?

Ned Corvan's song says so and that it was a French spy. Yet what of the Boddam wreckers' connection; the evidence of railway rivalry and Croft fishermen's disgruntlement; and the aquatic jenny haniver speculation? What of our knowledge of relocated folktales; the tradition of a stupid/commonsensical community motif? For what purpose did Corvan dress his song up in Napoleonic guise rather than direct railway rivalry?

Indeed, aren't we getting too academic anyway?

Seriously, does it matter at the end of the day whether a monkey was really hanged? There is plenty of raw data: names, places and dates. That's called history. There is also much tradition, contention and speculation. That's called myth.

It is a fallacy of conventional scholarship to distinguish between these aspects with rigorous discipline and distinction. For folklore is the psychic life of a people and cannot be separated artificially from shared events. Legends may seem like lies but they always have an element of truth. Even when exaggeration and embellishment are applied, even to the extent of deliberate falsification and invention, such "lies" of a people are not wholly gratuitous. They refer to some strata of communal reality where underlying fears, deficiencies, desires and dreams require exorcising or compensating. Their falsity makes them real; their power makes them true.

In this way a self-definition of a community is created; a collective identity occurs just when and where it is needed. It can be a truth without true tangibility.

So "Who hung the monkey, O!"

We did.

THE END

But what makes you think I'm a Frenchman?

PRINTABILITY PUBLISHING

present for your enjoyment an ever expanding collection of local interest books, prints, maps, videos and greetings cards.
Why not have a browse around our shop at:

Atkinson the Printer

10/11 Lower Church Street, Hartlepool, Cleveland TS24 7DJ
Telephone: 0429 267849   Fax: 0429 865416

BOOK TITLES

An Illustrated History of Wolviston Village by Adrian Liddell £2.75
Dawn Raid by John Ward £2.95
The Hartlepool Chronology by John Ward £4.95
Over the Gates by Jean Tabley £1.25
Back Over the Gates by Jean Tabley £2.00
Tate's Description of Hartlepool, Stranton and Seaton £1.25
Hutton Henry Village by John Etherington £5.95
Cleveland In Times Past by Paul Menzies £2.95
German Raid on the Hartlepools (Sage Stationer) £1.95
Lister Street School by Rob Wilson £1.50
Firm Favourites, Recipe Book by Sue Johnson £4.95
Shipbuilders of the Hartlepools by Bert Spaldin £5.95
Jackson's Town by Eric Waggott £4.00
History of Hartlepool by Cuthbert Sharp £5.50
West Hartlepool by Robert Wood £5.00
The Chick Henderson Story by Frank Wappat £5.95
An Illustrated History of Wynyard Estate by Adrian Liddell £2.95
The Hartlepool Story by Walter Gill .... £3.75 paperback   £8.00 hardback
Our Patch by John Etherington £3.50
A range of Doug Ferriday and George Colley Books .... from £3.60 — £7.95

PRINTS (full colour)

The Train Spotter, West Hartlepool Railway Station .... Mounted . £13.50 .... Framed £32.50
The Town Wall & Croft, Hartlepool .... Mounted £13.50 .... Framed £32.50
Scotland Pond, Wolviston .... Mounted . £13.50 .... Framed £32.50
Hartlepool Headland 1990 .... Framed £37.50
Healthful Hartlepool — Edwardian Poster Collection ... Print Only . £2.95 .... Framed £16.50
The Warrior by John Wigston .... Print Only   £4.50 .... Framed £37.50
The Wingfield Castle by John Wigston .... Print Only   £4.50 .... Framed £32.50
The Durham Map .... Framed £18.95

PRINTS (Black & White)

Opening of the West Hartlepool Docks, 1880 .... Framed £15.95
Durham Cathedral by N. Allen .... Framed £37.50
Durham Castle by N. Allen .... Framed £37.50
A selection of prints produced from original drawings based on old postcard scenes of Hartlepool from the early part of this century by Garry Courtnell...Framed £16.50 to £23.50

CHRISTMAS CARDS pack of 5 (singles available from the shop) plus envelopes

Elwick Village by Walter Parker £2.25
December In Dockland by Walter Parker £2.25
Derwentwater In December by Walter Parker £2.25
The Town Wall, Hartlepool by Stephen Crowther £2.95
St. Hilda's Church, Hartlepool by Stephen Crowther £2.95
Winter Wonderland, Ward Jackson Park Bandstand by Stan Suggitt £2.25
Scotland Pond, Wolviston by Darren Cairns £1.50
Middlegate, Hartlepool Headland, 1920's photograph .... Large £2.25   Small £1.50

VIDEOS

The Hartlepool Video (VHS only) £11.95
The Hartlepool Lifeboats (VHS only) £10.95

All the items mentioned can be ordered from Printability Publishing at the above address.
Please include 45p post and packing for books and Christmas cards, £1.50 for Chick Henderson, prints and Videos.
Our free catalogue is available on request and overseas enquiries are welcomed.
Prices correct 1st September, 1991.

THE CHICK HENDERSON STORY AND COMPLETE DISCOGRAPHY

by Frank Wappat

Read the life story about the meteoric rise to fame of a local lad, Chick Henderson.

His short recording career, spanning only 7 years from 1935-1942 saw him become Britains No. 1 singer, with timeless tunes such as "Zing went the Strings of my Heart" and the classic "Begin the Beguine" — the first dance record to sell **one million** copies.

PRICE ONLY £5.95
(includes FREE cassette of
Begin the Beguine/My Prayer)
or by post
(+ £1.50 post & packing)

An Illustrated History
of

WYNYARD
ESTATE
by
Adrian Liddell

Containing 64 pages and 70 illustrations, the book portrays the Estate in all its glory. Read of the Londonderry's reign and Estate life up the departure of the family in 1987 and the subsequent purchase of Wynyard by Sir John Hall, of Metro Centre fame.

(2nd impression July, 1991)
PRICE ONLY £2.95
or by post (+ 45p post & packing)

An Illustrated History
of

HARTBURN
VILLAGE
by
Robert Woodhouse

Written by popular local author Bob Woodhouse, the history of Hartburn looks at Village life from 1183 under William de Hertbourne (a descendent of George Washington) to its present day status as a pleasant residential suburb of Stockton-on-Tees.

PRICE £2.75